KARHUN OTSA

POEMS
by

Will Lahti
and
David William Salmela

Copyright © 1992 by
David William Salmela and
Will Lahti

ISBN No. 0-9632975-1-1

Cover design by David William Salmela

Layout by Weikko Järvi,
Työmies Society

Will first suggested a poetry challenge. We were immediately intrigued by the idea. We agreed upon a common subject and then each of us wrote a poem about that subject without comparing notes, or reading each other's poems.

Our first poetry challenge was to write about the Finnish built sauna at the new Salolampi Language Village site on Turtle River Lake near Bemidji, Minnesota. **The Sauna** and **new sauna poem** came from our first poetry challenge. It turned out to be so much fun that we decided to do another. We decided to write about a special tree for our next poetry challenge.

A dead elm had stood near the nuotio, just outside the ring of stones that surrounded the campfire, at Salolampi for many decades. This tree was a part of Salolampi life: we leaned on it, hid behind it and used it as a stage door for Kalevala skits. One spring when we were visiting Salolampi before camp, we saw that a storm had toppled the dead elm. **The Elm** and **dead elm poem** were the result of this second poetry challenge.

The third set of poems, **The Ancestors** and **wrestling with ghosts** came from a powerful first line of a poem Will was working on. I asked, "Hey, do you think we could use your first line as a poetry challenge?"

"Sure," Will replied.

"Are you sure you don't mind? I mean, after all, it's your first line and I wouldn't want you to feel uptight about me using it," I said.

"No, let's use it."

This third set of poems is our favorite. We are amazed at the similarities in feeling, word choice and action. We hope you enjoy reading them as much as we enjoyed writing them.

THE SAUNA

Gentle slap, slap, slap
   of waves on the stones of shore,
glimmers of reflected sun
   shine through the windowed door.
Watercolors swirled by twilight
   lend the lake its deep dark depths of night.

Steady slap, slap, slap
   of birch boughs tied with vine,
bowed head and sweat and
   breath of life entwined
with shimmers of heated stones
   atop the crackling stove.

Ssk hiss, ssk hiss, ssk hiss
   of steam and heat that rise
to mist the windows over and
   hide the world outside.
Firmly, naked feet find the floor,
   warmth and chill mingle at the door…

from the warmth of womb—reborn!
   Steady slap, slap, slap
of feet across the waves.
   Emerald water soothes the heated core.
Dive and surface; turn to look: Mother of Life!
   the sauna beckoning from the shore.

                        — David William Salmela

new sauna poem

weeds in the lake coil
around my ankles and seem to
tug like the hand of ahto
but i do not wish to sleep
face down on the black-ooze bottom.

sun just above the treeline
does not warm me so i swim back
to shore where i can see
the sauna through my blurry eyes.

— Will Lahti

THE ELM

The fire is contained within a ring of stones,
    held in by the horizon of dusk.

An ugly man stands with his back to the flame.
    His tall-boned silhouette dances on the leaves
    of summer trees,
    stock still he stands.

The twilight dies, stars glow, the moon wavers
    in the flaming river.

The dead of night arrives.
The fire dies away.

The ugly man grows larger—
    stretching toward the moon.
    His long fingers are slender twigs.
    His feet are roots that hold his
    deadened body still; unmoving.
    His skin flakes, peeling loosely
    revealing bleached bones.

Embers turn to ash.
The wind rises.
The storm arrives.
Ashes turn to mud.
Fingers supplicating
entwine with lightning.
The bones come crashing.
The mud dries.
Clearing clouds at daybreak
find him broken on the ground.

dead elm poem

alveoli stretching skyward
for shimmering air and stars
twigs clawing and grasping
like boney death's fingers
looking more like roots than
branches in the dark soil of night
i watch from my mole eyes
flat on my back quite blind.

THE ANCESTORS

With every dipper of water
  that hits the smooth,
  hot rocks
  another ancestor joins me
  on the top bench.

Scorching blast after blast
  slaps my backside.
  Sweat beads and drips.
  I exhale forcefully and
  wipe the stinging salt from my eyes.

The top bench grows crowded.
  Water scorches off the glowing stove pipe.
  It's too hot.
  It's too crowded.
  I step down.
  The Ancients glare silently,
  dead eyes pierce sauna's hot vapors.

I stand in front of the fogged pane
  of the window separating this world
  from the other.
  I reach to wipe the glass clear
  so I can see out.
    Hot sweat mixes with cool condensation,
    rivulets run tracks of the past.
    Over my shoulder I hear the steady breathing
    of the generations.

Outside; the unborn gaze longingly in.
  Body after body of future generations
  wait stoicly in line
  to take steam with The Ancients,
  with whom, I am now one.

wrestling with ghosts

with every dipper of water
that hits the smooth hot rocks
another ancestor joins me
on the top bench.
we are drawn without explanation
or struggle towards our fate.
through trial and tribulation
emotion may not be shown.

steam recedes from the window
and i see rye being sown in
huhta field, ash and brown earth
full of promise, coming winter's bread.
another dipperful and yet another
silent ancient joins me and
the scene in the window
is obscured with mist.

scorching wave makes me grimace.
sweat stings my eyes but i
won't be the first to step down.
bear hardship in silent determination.
they won't budge but i can't
step down. the wood handled
dipper belongs in my hands. my
 time is now.

three quick splashes and the
ancients grumble. two more
and nothing remains of them
but hot stones.
the window clears and i see the
future bearing armloads of wood and
buckets of water. i suppose they'll
be wanting the dipper.

II

For a hobby I stack stones into free-standing structures. I have built them everywhere I go. I once stacked a stone pile in Oulu, Finland. After I had returned home I thought about that stone pile and wrote **Stone Atop Stone.**

The rest of the poems in this section deal with my initial feelings upon arriving in Oulu and subsequent observations of my Finnishness through changes in the seasons.

— David William Salmela

STONE
ATOP
STONE

Stone
   atop
  Stone
sturdy and solid.
Blue sky above
dark earth below.
At night,
the moon or stars.
At dawn,
the sun and morning star
     still stand
     stone
     stand
     still.

SUOMI

foreign land, the sun and sky,
the moon and stars at night.
foreign soil, the ancestral cry
to heed; place of my father's,
father's, father's birth.
        gathering impressions cast
in the bed of damp soil—
fleeting prints of my heritage.
hold true, never falter
homeland of my beginning.
mother forest,
father sky,
sister dearest,
brother mine,
hand in hand in hand
to that final place,
to that foreign land.

DEAD MOON

salolammen kuu
    shines unerringly
    upon this space of earth
    somewhere between
    summer and autumn,
    somewhere between
    death's heavy hurts
    and life's empty hearse.

    no grave to be buried in
    no steady cemetery
    no stones to call
    my own.

ICE CANDLES

Ice candles glowing
  through the dark
  of night,

      diffusing shadows,
      casting warmth to the eye.
        Silent stars wheel
        the cold streak
        of a falling star
        tears the sky
        like a wooden match
        being struck on
        the canopy of night.

SUO

I am reminded of the deep, penetrating
stillness of the winter's night—
    snow absorbs the sounds,
    but leaves the silence
    pounding.

Dark, still sky.
Light, still snow.
Stark trees shadow the luminescence.
Here and there a
finger of a branch
thrusts out from the snow
cautions me to be still.

There could be no freezing to death tonight
as the blood courses.

  The stillness
  is as far from harshness
     as the wind is
     from tangling the bulrushes—
     rustling above the frozen marsh,
  from the snow itself
  shifting from
   place
      to place.

BONDS

winter's endless
  breath is blown

          summer's distance
            lengthened

bitter chill
  again made known

          bonds of ice are
            strengthened

LEIPÄJUUSTO

I learn.
Standing silently looking over my shoulder
are my ancestors. Looking over their shoulders
are more ancestors and ancestors and ancestors
all nodding in approval, gently correcting me if I err
and upon completion
I reach out with my twine and
twist it gently among the living rope of history
that stretches eternally past.
Empowered at last.
Given the right to complete the circle
only if I guarantee that I will stand behind
someone's shoulder and gently, approvingly
look on.

III

As I see it, part of Finnishness is the influence of nature in my poems. Many of my inspirations come from the natural world. Particularly interesting to me is the last poem in this section, **Silver Lady**, which is inspired by the oxygenated waves foaming as they break on the rocky shoreline of Lake Superior.

THREE

Three birches; no leaves.
    An old one,
    a young one,
    a sapling.

Three lives; many loves.
    A new one,
    a mature one,
    motherly.

Three directions; all growing.
    Inwardly,
    outwardly,
    slowly.

Three loves; one base.
    of self,
    of mate,
    maternal.

This base is love.
    Strong.
    Caring.
    Sure.

TWILIGHT

Black spruce
like paintbrushes
sweep away the day.
The mists
like sponges
absorb the points
of trees.
The moon
so full
accentuates
the packages
of fog
individually wrapped
around each low swamp
each low slue hole.

SWAMP SESTINA

In the dark cold water
stretch and wave the grasses,
pushed and rolled by the wind
that passes by the sun.
The mire is dank and chill
within this murky marsh.

The songbird of the marsh
sings across the water,
floating above the chill
by clutching to the grasses.
Red winged blackbird; in sun
and song, rocks with the wind.

Ceaselessly howls the wind
to far edges of the marsh.
Distantly shines the sun.
Blackbird flies from water.
Shivers spread through thegrasses
as if struck by sodden chill...

as if pressed with sudden chill.
And now the bitter wind
is whipping the grasses.
The action of the marsh
is violent and the water
dazzles frothing to the sun.

Clouds are hiding the sun.
The brute strength of the chill
tries to freeze the water.
The howling screaming wind
pushes life from the marsh
and tries flattening the grasses.

But resilient grasses
wait until the warm sun
blazes into the marsh
dispersing bitter chill,
until the wind is warm wind
rippling across the water.

So the marsh absorbed the chill
while grasses absorbed the sun.
What's left is wind and water.

TWILIGHT

grey to grey,
mist to darkness,
embalmed in
charcoal waters .

Figures of trees
sentinels of
the forest,
melding greyness
to the earth.

SILVER LADY

a silver lady
  by the shore
    provoking waves
      to come bask
        in the summer
          sun with me for
            awhile the waves
              say slip beneath
            emerald doors
          with light diffused
        and undone
      waves touching the
    shore provoking the
silver lady to come

IV

This last section of poems deals with a journey to the Harvala farm where I spent much of my youth. I begin this journey in the small town of Menagha, Minnesota where a midsummer celebration is held each year. After that I travel to the farm where I am lost in recollection and emotion. Finally, at the end of this section, I leave my youthful memories behind in **The Yellow Barn**.

MENAGHA MIDSUMMER JUHLA

Ain't life great, though?
Dead rat on the road.
The black plague
doing no harm.
Sun's warm
on
my
backside.
Long walk there
where the cool pines'
height breathes peace and
the pancake feed commences...

SIBELIUS

I was driving in my car.
Public Radio quietly
filled the chamber.
   And then a chord resounded!
   A refrain so pure!
      Depth of vision
      increased with volume
      and the city faded.

      Cement center-islands
      became the archipelago.
      Glinting chrome bumpers
      were the dazzling
      diamonds of sun
      glimmering on the water.

Sibelius swelled
the chamber of my heart.

THE WAY IT WORKS

At the farmplace
   I sit in the musty chair.
      I watch dustmotes shine.
      A stale recollection
    washes over me.

I sit in the chair.
   I am at the juncture
     of past and present;
       recollection—sweet unction,
         intervention of spirit.
          I trace the patterns
          in the armrest:
             this is the connection—
             the physical touching—
             that opens the floodgates
               of stale cereal,
               muddy coffee
               and voices echoing
               up the stairs.

PUKKI

once when the snow fell
I thought that
I saw a pukki
I aimed
my BIG GUN and
then I pulled
the trigger
and
Hugo B. laughed
as I fell over
backwards

KEINUTUOLI

. . . pointless and endless
then the rocking chair
embraces and confines a life
of mess and havoc in its
wooden arms and feet.
    creak, creak, creak
    back and forth
    only one toe
    propelling the craft
    into older age.
chair creaks,
bones creak,
    floor underneath snaps,
    knuckles beneath skin crack
and then the rocking chair embraces
reaffirming endless and pointless . . .

DRAWING

All that I did was draw
   the drawknife
      in slow, smooth strokes
         through the bark of the severed limb.
           Curls of dead bark fell at my feet and
         the scent of peeled tree reached
      inside me.

It felt good to do this in the twilight:
   a half-moon visible in the overhead
   and a half-smile on my lips.

THE COW POND

The laughter is past.
Only the markings from
the blades leave
a trace of
what was.

The snow is heaped
in trampled piles.
Frozen moments
cannot be unfrozen.
The dead
cannot come
to life.

After awhile the spring comes.
The traces of the blades
melt into the sheen
atop the ice,
the ice melts into the pond
and the rest will be gone.

AFTER SAUNA

Triangle of light ever-widening,
steam ever-rising.
Line of light from the door
made visible by tendrils of steam
rising from my heated body —
rising through the pale yellow glow,
disappearing from view
when the strong darkness
of the cold night
obliterates its passing.

Beneath my feet the cold seeps,
chilling the joints of my knees.
My backside is hot from sauna's heat.

Triangle of light ever-narrowing
in proportionate degrees
until the door shudders to a close.
The darkness is complete.
No artificial light reaches
the retina of my brain.

I sit on the ground
feeling sticks and particles
of leaves adhere
to my bottom.
I sit until
the dew-wet dirt
is less comforting
than the thought of
pie and coffee.

THE YELLOW BARN

The yellow barn smells like
old oil and rusted stanchions.
Broken hinges hold the ladder
leading to the loft.

Scraping shovels push manure
and old straw down the gutters.
The tabby cat yawns for warm milk
drinks from a teat stream.
I hear echoes of Finnish words
speaking in my brain
bent backs sitting on
handmade stools, "Tu, lehemä, tu."

Dustmotes float in
broken panes of sunshine.
Past panes, the door opens.
Cobwebs drift on gossamer wings.

My car door slams. Tires roll.
The dust rises to the sun.
It settles slowly, my lonesome
tracks are covered.

While I was living in Duluth's Central Hillside neighborhood, Pat McKinnon suggested that I explore my own history as material for my poetry. This suggestion inevitably led me to my past and to the experiences of my family as Finnish Americans.

My roots run deep. I have been influenced by the swamps of Field Township, the sandy soil of Embarrass, the Yliniemi farm near Pickeral Lake, and the red dirt of Marengo. The spirit of my family is in all of these places. With faith in our hearts we make our way through this world.

I dedicate these poems to all Finnish Americans.

—Will Lahti

origins

i found these poems scattered
along the path through the spruce bog.

i found these poems growing
beneath birch trees by the sauna.

these poems were rooted
in pastures fringed by thistles.

these poems were pulled
from boulder choked fields.

berry picking

we wandered through the yellow-crowned
birches towards the swamp and its cloud
of black spruce hovering over a universe
of shimmering blueberry planets.

the tips of our fingers turned dirty blue
as if they were wrapped in rubberbands
waiting to fall off but it was only the
sweet-tasting blood of the frosted globes.

as the berries rained a song against the
bottoms of our buckets she told me who i
was and she told me where i came from
then she sang a picture for me.

the words were of her father kalle who
was my great-grandfather and they sounded like
horses pulling a plow through healthy
topsoil never striking stones.

kalle and his brothers would row their
boat to a pair of rocks covered with
lichen scales like fish in the kiiminki
river to play church.

the pappi would preach from the higher
rock with the congregation assembled on
the lower slicing onions below their eyes
making tears showing that the
holy ghost had arrived.

hunting grouse

green flutterings shimmer
in my ears underneath the
pockmarked dusty trunks of aspen.

i push my silver offering for
tapio's daughter into the crumbling
flesh of a pine stump.

i walk down the mossy trail
and breathe in deep the always
earthy decay of the forest.

across brown clay waters of the
pond a spruce drops spiraling cardinals
wings singing in a whisper.

family tradition

when great-grandfather was 4 years old
he and his brother would play funeral.

since matti was the youngest
he had to be the corpse.

he played this role so well that
one day his brothers buried him alive.

central hillside

look out your window
in a grey downtown day
at the lake brown-green
angry moss boiling.

water swelling slightly at
the farthest shore red-black
with the smell of iron
on the horizon.

walking along third street
old kaarlo is on a drunk
again broken wobblie
dreams carve lines in his
face straining against the
hint of desolation in the wind.

ecochauvinism

when i was six
ross anderson and i
taught the neighbor lady's dog
to fetch rocks.

it was fun to throw them in the lake
black lab almost drowning
in its eagerness to retrieve.

apostolic

kids didn't have to
be in the church during
services until confirmation
at fourteen so church
was fun.

we'd dig big holes in the
sand outside trying to
catch cars when we were
little or throw snowballs
at the outhouse.

echoes of song would
reach our football game
in the field and
we'd rush inside for a communion
of kool-aid and flatbread.

the hole in his soul

was as obvious to me
as the gaping maw of
mister saarinen's
empty eye socket
during our 7th grade woodshop
safety-goggle lecture.

almost all of her neighbors spoke finnish

even the kids, she remembered riding to school
in the horse-drawn school bus which
was driven by a man who could not speak finnish.

he felt pretty stupid when he couldn't understand
their jibber jabber so he decided to fix those
little foreign devils.

he hung up a sign in the front of the bus
that said: this is america
speak english.

embarrass, mn

5 year old july summer at gramma johnson's
my cousins and i drinking gold medal strawberry
while mashing grasshoppers in an arco coffee can
passing time until an aunt or uncle would
take us to wiitala's for a swim.

grandpa's nameless finger

while sawing through white pine logs
on a bright march morning
great grandfather let the balmy
false spring weather distract him.

with an arc of blood spraying a
pattern in the snow that looked
like a superior red's hammer and sickle
he cut his finger off.

lännentie

it was late october and the
fall rains had come to an end
the leaves on the trees blazed
with as much brilliance as
the indian summer sun
in blue finnish sky.

soon would be november
eventually resulting in snow
but first the leaves would drop
and fade just as the sun
would lose some of its glory
in the northern winter.

a letter from aunt esther

DEAR WILL

its a beautiful day here in pike lake
your uncle Jalmer is out castrating the pigs
so tell me, is there a special girl in your life?

song of worms

with hands of sin i
tear a fist-full from the
earth and cram it into
my reluctant mouth chewing
crunching grinding teeth impervious
to tiny glacial pebbles.

soil and sand clog my throat
with breathless terror i want to
cry out then up from my guts
over my tongue past my lips
the song of worms comes screaming
damp loamy darkness.

i wonder sometimes

whatever happened to
old mrs. jukola and
then i remember bill lindquist
and how he thought his dinosaur
pencil sharpener was alive and
then i think of how the class turtle
ate all the frogs that we had hoped
would be its best friends.

sound advice

don't play near the
wringer washer said
old mrs. reed it'll
catch your fingers
and pull you through
its cylindrical
lips crushing you
with kisses.

about northern blood

the sudden chill of the late december
afternoon compels me to retrace my
steps and head back to the woodstove
kitchen and steaming coffee.
the snow that managed to wedge
itself in the tops of my pike river
oxfords is now ice and resists
the efforts of my gloved fingers.

i come to a tangle of blown-over trees
and brush snow off one that looks
like a nice place to sit and inhale the
living cold each breath of the sparkling
quiet draws images from my subconscious
and i exhale them in steamy clouds
of vapor and crystals that look like forever.

the sun sends its last orange
streaks to my watery eyes through
winter's deciduous bones
cast off whitetail antlers rattling
the land will be with me as long as
northern blood flows through my
veins leaving traces of its song
at the tip of my tongue.

dusk comes with a raven's wings
as he lands on an ash snag
that points skyward to the
everpresent peg of the heavens
with this in mind i rise and continue
homeward where i know thet evening
sky shines winter blue over the aspen
borders of snow crust field.

NORMANDALE COMMUNITY COLLEGE
LIBRARY
9700 FRANCE AVENUE SOUTH
BLOOMINGTON, MN 55431-4399